MURDEROUS MATHS.

Professor Fiendish's
BOOK OF DIABOLICAL BRAINBENDERS

Completely written by Professor Fiendish
with <u>no</u> help at all from

KJARTAN POSKITT

(in fact I've never heard of him)

Illustrated by Philip Reeve

D0336931

I1776005

JOIN THE PROFESSOR AND THE REST OF THE MURDEROUS MATHS GANG FOR MORE FUN, GAMES AND TIPS ON WWW.MURDEROUSMATHS.CO.UK.

Scholastic Children's Books,
Commonwealth House, 1–19 New Oxford Street,
London WC1A 1NU, UK

A division of Scholastic Ltd
London ~ New York ~ Toronto ~ Sydney ~ Auckland
Mexico City ~ New Delhi ~ Hong Kong

Published in the UK by Scholastic Ltd, 2002

Text copyright © Kjartan Poskitt 2002
Illustrations copyright © Philip Reeve 2002

All rights reserved

ISBN 0 439 98226 X

Typeset by Falcon Oast Graphic Art Ltd.
Printed and bound in Finland by WS Bookwell

2 4 6 8 10 9 7 5 3 1

The right of Kjartan Poskitt and Philip Reeve to be identified
as the author and illustrator of this work respectively has been asserted by them in accordance with the
Copyright, Designs and Patents Act, 1988.

SANDWELL LIBRARY & INFORMATION SERVICE		
I1776005		
Cypher		21.12.02
J793.7		£5.99

This book is sold subject to the condition that it shall not, by way of trade or otherwise be lent, resold,
hired out, or otherwise circulated without the publisher's prior consent in any form or binding other than
that in which it is published and without a similar condition, including this condition, being imposed upon
the subsequent purchaser.

So what have I got lined up for you, eh? If you've read the *Murderous Maths* books then you'll have already seen how my contributions bring a badly needed splash of style, wit and genius to the world of publishing. It was only a matter of time before the MM Organization *begged* me to produce this modest little offering which I call my *Diabolical Brainbenders*. There's loads of my favourite teasers and puzzles in here and you'll also find I was kind enough to let the lesser *Murderous Maths* stars appear occasionally.

Er, OK, I admit it, I've got a pet pig. But just because she can talk, it doesn't mean she makes sense so just ignore her. Now turn the page and look at the contents list...

Contents

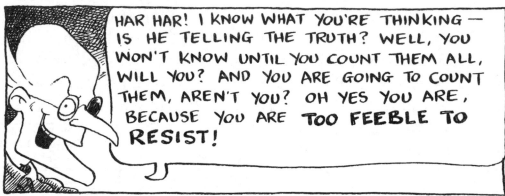

HAR HAR! I KNOW WHAT YOU'RE THINKING — IS HE TELLING THE TRUTH? WELL, YOU WON'T KNOW UNTIL YOU COUNT THEM ALL, WILL YOU? AND YOU ARE GOING TO COUNT THEM, AREN'T YOU? OH YES YOU ARE, BECAUSE YOU ARE **TOO FEEBLE TO RESIST!**

8   The start of the DEVIOUS BRAINBENDERS section.
Obviously it's going to be a bit tragic for you trying to match your
puny brain against mine, so to make it a bit easier for you I've
split the book into three sections: Devious, Drastic and Diabolical.
You might manage to solve a few of the Devious Brainbenders,
but if you manage to solve *any* of the Drastic Brainbenders you
may call yourself a genius. As for the Diabolical Brainbenders –
you won't get any of these right, I just put them in to show how
clever I am. You can read them but don't even dream of trying
to find the answers or your head will melt. Har har!

The MYSTERY TOUR

IF YOU GET BORED TURNING THE PAGES OVER ONE AT A TIME, YOU CAN GO A BIT WILD AND FOLLOW THE CLUES TO THE MYSTERY TOUR!

Each clue on the tour gives you a number as the answer. If you turn to that numbered page, you'll find another clue at the bottom which sends you to another page and so on. You also score points as you go along, and each clue tells you how to update your score. The tour ends on page 58... Oh go on, have a quick look, you know you want to. But COME STRAIGHT BACK HERE.

Welcome back. Now as you can see, you'll need to know what your exact final score should be, so keep your brains on red alert!

- If you get to a page that has *no* clue then you've gone wrong!
- If you end up going round the same pages again and again then you've gone wrong!
- If the score update makes your score negative or into a fraction then you've gone wrong!

Here's your first clue:

Mystery Tour

A rectangular floor is exactly covered in square tiles. If there are 20 tiles round the edge, what is the largest number of tiles there could be altogether? (Work it out then turn to that page...)

The DEVIOUS Brainbenders

> HERE'S A FEW QUICK LITTLE TEASERS TO START YOU OFF BEFORE YOU GET TO THE MAIN PUZZLES.

> IF YOU CAN'T DO THESE — OH DEAR, OH DEARY ME!

1 Look at the digits 1 2 3 4. If you put in an = sign and a × you get this sum: 12 = 3 × 4. Can you find another set of four consecutive digits that you can do this to?

2 A normal newspaper is supposed to have 60 pages, but pages 24 and 41 are missing. Which other pages won't be there?

3 Can you put three + signs and one – sign in with these digits to make the sum work? 9 8 7 6 5 4 3 2 1 = 100 (For example you could put 9 + 87 – 6 + 543 + 21 but that would come to 654 so it'd be wrong.)

4 A CD player and a battery for it cost £101 together. The CD player costs £100 more than the battery. What does the battery cost?

5 When I got to the station platform, the clock read 09:49. My train was due at 09:58. I noticed that if you added the digits of each time together you got 0 + 9 + 4 + 9 = 22 and also 0 + 9 + 5 + 8 = 22. As it turns out, the train was delayed and I had to wait until the *next* time that the digits added up to 22 before the train arrived. How late was the train?

6 Two whole numbers multiplied together make 100,000. If neither of them end in 0, what are they?

7 Pongo McWhiffy has a dial on his bike to show how many miles he has travelled. This morning it read 7112. He set off to collect his washing from his Aunt Aroma, but when he'd got back home he realized that his clean pants had fallen out of the  bag. He pedalled back to find them lying in a smelly puddle so he squeezed them out and then came home again. When he got home the dial read 7134. If it's 7 miles from his house to Aunt Aroma's, how far is it from Aunt Aroma's to the puddle?

8 What is eleven million plus eleven thousand plus eleven hundred plus eleven?

9 There's a family where the girls have the same number of brothers as sisters but the boys have twice as many sisters as brothers. How many of each are there?

10 Which of these do you think is the biggest item you could cover with one million £1 coins?
a) an elephant   **b)** a school hall floor
c) a football pitch **d)** Dundee

11 You can divide the number 1274953680 exactly by *any* number from 1 to 16. But can you see anything else special about it? (Don't do any sums, just look at it!)

12 7997 is a "palindromic" number, which means that it's the same forwards as it is backwards. If you count upwards from 7997, what is the next palindrome you get? Now try it with 41314 and with 99999.

The Romantic Roses

I've always got a soft spot for the romantic type, and that's why I was delighted to help Pongo McWhiffy in his quest to impress the terribly lovely Veronica Gumfloss ... har har! Here's what Pongo wanted:

- Two roses with long stems and two roses with short stems.
- Two roses with red petals and two roses with white petals.
- At least one rose with a long stem *and* white petals.
- Two roses without long stems.
- Two roses without any white petals.
- At least one rose with a short stem *and* red petals.
- Two roses without short stems.
- Two roses without any red petals.

Of course, I was only too happy to oblige, and like a good boy Pongo paid me for 18 roses. I even delivered them for him just as he'd ordered.

 The seventh living person to touch the bottle must drink the poison, so if Ffarg started the game, Gorgo would have been first to drink.

10

Ten Tantalizing Cards

Get the ace, 2, 3, 4, 5, 6, 7, 8, 9 and 10 of a pack of cards. Can you lay them out face down like this to make a squarish shape?

Have you managed it? Well done, aren't you clever? Yes, of course you are.

But just to make it a *little* bit harder, can you now lay the same ten cards in the same pattern face up, so that the three cards on the top row add up to 18? (The ace counts as 1.) Oh, and the three cards on the bottom row have to add up to 18 too. And so do the four cards up the left-hand side *and* so do the four cards up the right-hand side!

And if you haven't got cards, look at these eight dominoes:

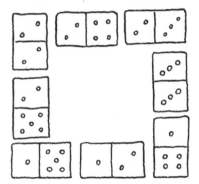

You'll see the top and bottom sides of the square have 13 spots each. Can you rearrange the dominoes so that *all* four sides of the square have 13 spots each?

HAR HAR! NOT FEELING SO CLEVER NOW, ARE YOU?

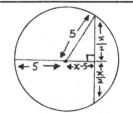

Call the length of each ladder x. If you draw in a radius of the circle (which is 5 m long) you get a right-angled triangle. Then if you know about Pythagoras' theorem, and a bit of algebra you can get the answer!

Calculator Hunting

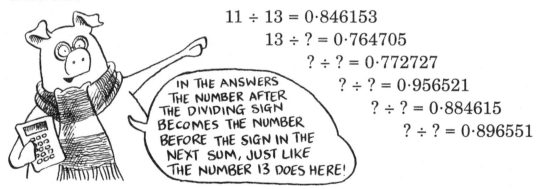

If you put 11 ÷ 13 into a calculator what do you get? If you try it you'll see 0·846153 on the display. (We'll only bother with the first six digits for this game.)

But suppose you were told the answer was 0·846153 and you had to find out which two numbers you need to divide to make it: that's calculator hunting!

Can you find which numbers to divide to make the following answers:

$$11 \div 13 = 0·846153$$
$$13 \div ? = 0·764705$$
$$? \div ? = 0·772727$$
$$? \div ? = 0·956521$$
$$? \div ? = 0·884615$$
$$? \div ? = 0·896551$$

IN THE ANSWERS THE NUMBER AFTER THE DIVIDING SIGN BECOMES THE NUMBER BEFORE THE SIGN IN THE NEXT SUM, JUST LIKE THE NUMBER 13 DOES HERE!

Here's another calculator game:

Suppose you can only use the 7, 8, 9 and the + − ×÷ = buttons... What's the fastest way to make these numbers appear on your screen: 5   25   50   100 ?

Mystery Tour

SCORE UPDATE: Reverse the digits of your score!

NEXT CLUE: Can you find a two-digit number that divides by 6 and is 10 times as big as the two digits added together?

The Meter Cheater

Have you ever admired how much money people put into parking meters? I have, and that's why I've put a few *extra* parking meters round the town in the most inconvenient places. And in some places my meters are only a metre apart! They are all connected up to underground pipes so that the money falls into my secret vault.

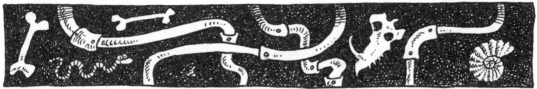

There's twice as much money from the hospital car-park meters as there is from the meters by the school gates. The meters by the petrol pumps have collected as much as the school meters and the meters by the station together. The meters by the station have £20 less than the school metres.

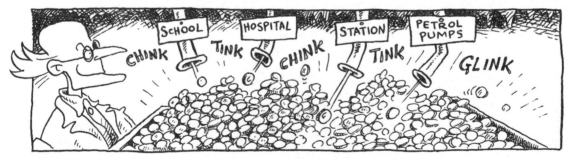

Which meters collect the smallest amount of money and which collect the most? If the metres by the petrol pumps have collected £100, how much money have all the metres collected together?

 You don't need to find out exactly what a Motley or a Prof is worth!

The Serpent Stones

Don't you just hate it when you're watching the telly and can't find the remote control? Especially when you're on a desert island, and you suddenly realize that for no good reason, the remote control is on *another* desert island? Quick! Before that four-hour documentary on civil-service expenditure melts your soul, you've got to cross the stepping stones … but be careful! There's a serpent in the water who's extremely desperate for you  to fall in. You must only step on the stones linked by the dotted lines because these are the shallow bits where the serpent doesn't like hiding.

I bet you think it looks easy, don't you? (And yes, you can step on the funny shaped stones if you like. They are just there to make it pretty.)

The tricky bit is that the stones are so small, you can only put one foot on each one. When you set off you have to put your left foot on the first stone, then your right foot on the next and then your left and so on. When you reach the other side you must have your right foot on the last stone so you can step safely ashore.

Can you find a way over the water?

And if you *do* manage to get your remote control, can you get back the other way starting with your right foot and finishing on your left?

Mystery Tour

SCORE UPDATE: Multiply by 3.

NEXT CLUE: You have a chequered board measuring 9 x 9 squares. You mark a cross on all the squares on both diagonals and all the squares round the edge. How many unmarked squares are left?

The Nasty Sur-prizes!

Look at these lovely prizes – can you see one you fancy? How about those thick woolly socks, they look warm, don't they? (They should be warm because I've just taken them off.) And doesn't that doughnut look succulent? It's succulent because I *lent* it to somebody and they *sucked* all the sugar off it. So come on, surely there is something you like on my prize stall!

You've got two exciting ways to win...

16

The Security Grid

ONE OF MY FAVOURITE THINGS IS MY SET OF SECRET NUMBERS! I'VE GOT ACCOUNT NUMBERS, PADLOCK NUMBERS AND LOADS OF OTHERS, AND THEY ARE ALL HIDDEN ON THIS SECURITY GRID — EITHER HORIZONTALLY, DIAGONALLY OR VERTICALLY, FORWARDS OR BACKWARDS! NONE OF THE NUMBERS ON THE GRID OVERLAP EACH OTHER AND, IN ALL THE NUMBERS, THE FIRST DIGIT IS SMALLER THAN THE LAST. I BET YOU CAN'T FIND THEM ALL!

- The four digits in my cash point number are all different and all in numerical order (but not consecutive such as 4567).
- The four digits in my fake passport number add up to 7.
- My Belgian post-office reserve account number has six digits all of which are different.
- The four digits of my bicycle padlock number are all different and don't include 4 or 7.
- The five digits in my fridge safe combination number add up to 34.
- If you reverse my shed number you get the answer to $1 \times 2 \times 3 \times 4 \times 5 \times 6$.

PAGE 80

Bolt Cutters

NOW FOR A REALLY TOUGH PUZZLE! A WEEDY PAPER AND PENCIL WON'T BE ANY GOOD TO YOU. INSTEAD YOU'LL NEED SOME HEAVY CHAINS AND SOME BOLT CUTTERS !

KERSNIK!

KERSNAK!

YOU NEED TO CHOP THE CHAINS UP AS INSTRUCTED, AND ALWAYS TRY TO MAKE THE NEW CHAINS AS LONG AS POSSIBLE. ANY LINKS YOU CHOP THROUGH ARE USELESS AND HAVE TO BE THROWN AWAY.

SUPPOSE YOU HAVE A CHAIN OF 13 LINKS AND WANT TO MAKE 3 CHAINS THE SAME LENGTH...

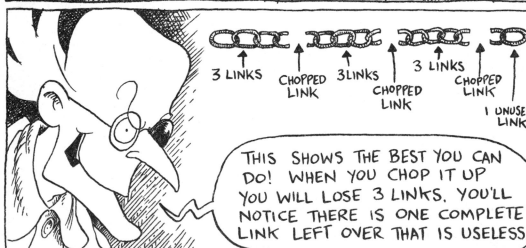

3 LINKS

CHOPPED LINK

3 LINKS

CHOPPED LINK

3 LINKS

CHOPPED LINK

1 UNUSED LINK

THIS SHOWS THE BEST YOU CAN DO! WHEN YOU CHOP IT UP YOU WILL LOSE 3 LINKS, YOU'LL NOTICE THERE IS ONE COMPLETE LINK LEFT OVER THAT IS USELESS.

Mystery Tour

SCORE UPDATE: Divide by 15.

NEXT CLUE: If corners score 2 points and edges score 1, what does a cube score?

18

Now chop your way through this lot and find out how long the new chains are…

a) Start with a chain of 22 links and make 4 chains the same length.

b) Make a 33 link chain into 3 chains the same length and one that's twice as long.

c) Chop a 32 link chain into 2 chains the same length and one chain that's 4 links longer.

d) Chop a 36 link chain into 3 chains – the second is twice the length of the first and the third is half the length of the first.

e) Make a 38 link chain into 5 chains, each of which is one link longer than the last one.

There, now wasn't that easy? I do hope you were doing that properly with your chains and a bolt cutter, because that makes the last bit of the problem very simple for you. If you look around the floor you'll see lots of chopped up links, but also some useless links that were not chopped! All I want to know is how many intact links you've got lying around on the floor.

OF COURSE IF YOU GOT ALL THESE ANSWERS WITH A PENCIL AND PAPER YOU'LL HAVE TO WORK THEM OUT ALL OVER AGAIN, WON'T YOU? HAR HAR!

Look at the table numbered '2'. As all the tables have a different number of cockroaches under them, the two tables on either side cannot both have 1 cockroach, so one must have 0 and one must have 2. If the table next to it numbered '17' had 0 cockroaches underneath it, then there would have to be 13 cockroaches under the table on the other side of the '13'. However, the maximum number of cockroaches is 12, therefore the 2 cockroaches must be under the '17' table and the zero must be under the '14' table. That's enough to get you started!

The Ravenous Rajah

It's time to take a break and sample the sophisticated cuisine and elegant surroundings of The Ravenous Rajah. It's a special night because Kumar is serving up his face-frazzling "Killer Curry". The menu is nice and simple.

Kumar's Killer Curry is simply the most yummy meal ever invented even if it does tend to scorch the pattern off the plates. Obviously you'll want to eat as many dishes of it as possible, but be warned:

- For every dish of curry you eat, you'll need at least one and a half bowls of ice cream to cool your face down and restore your powers of speech.
- The ice cream is a bit gooey, so you'll need three drinks for every ice cream you eat to wash it down.

If you've got a maximum of £12 to spend, how many plates of Killer Curry can you get through?

And if the Killer Curry hasn't filled you up, brace yourself for...

Pongo's Deluxe Burger Bar

Trade has been brisk today, and Pongo has made a list of what each customer paid him. If each victim … er, I mean *customer* had a drink, a burger and one extra item, can you work out which item *nobody* had?

 First work out how many years are between Granny and Drusilla, then work out their ages in the picture.

The Laboratory Shelf

If you've been wondering what the secret of my good looks is, it's my elixir of everlasting life which I drink daily. It's made up from very special ingredients, but to stop anybody just wandering in and mixing up a brew, the bottles aren't labelled.

- The Frog Spawn isn't in the middle and has a lower number than the Ant Blood.
- The Worm Juice is on the lower shelf but not next to the Otter Sweat, which is directly under the Ant Blood.
- The Pig Dribble is numbered two less than the Otter Sweat. Can you work out where the Fox Scent is?

Charity Day

Wah! I looked out of my skylight this morning and what did I see? The streets were crawling with gorillas, clowns, giant teddy bears, aliens, clowns, fairy princesses, cowboys, clowns and more clowns. For a moment I thought I'd woken into a hideous nightmare, but no – it was worse! It was CHARITY DAY. They were all out waving their little tins and buckets expecting me to pay them just for looking ridiculous. Bah! Nobody ever paid me for looking ridiculous.

Normally I wouldn't venture out until they'd gone, but sadly last week I dropped half a gorgonzola and kipper sandwich on the other side of town and the tantalizing aroma is driving me mad.

Here's a map of where they all stand and how much they charge you to get past them. Can you show me how to get to my drool-inducing sandwich without having to spend more than £10?

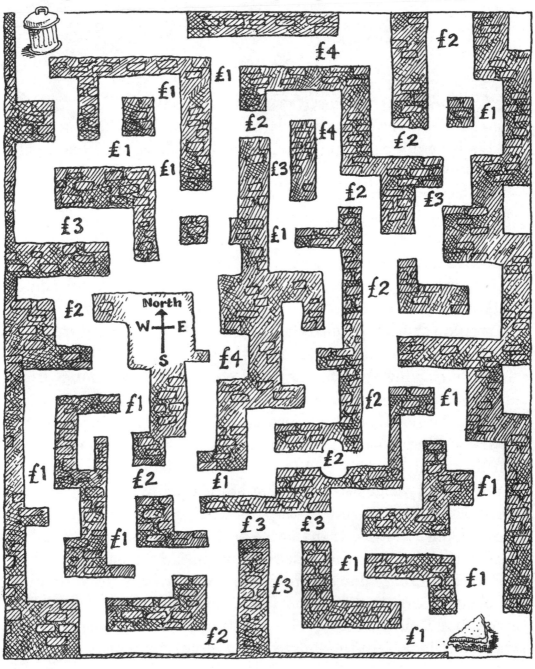

The Stake Out

City: **Chicago, Illinois, U.S.A.**
Place: **An empty basement room**
Date: **3 June 1928**
Time: **10:30 a.m.**

Seven shady men were hunched over a small table studying a map.

"This is gonna be a tough one," said Blade Boccelli. "Real tough. Needs careful planning."

"OK, so it's tough," said Half-smile. "But what is it?"

"It's at Goldtopps department store," said Blade. "That's all you need to know."

"Are we taking out the wages van?" asked Weasel.

"Or kidnapping old Ma Goldtopp?" suggested One Finger Jimmy.

Blade gulped. He knew he'd have to tell them sooner or later.

"I wouldn't normally ask you to do this, but..." he faltered.

"But what?" they all chorused.

"It's Dolly Snowlip's birthday and she wants poyf-yoom," Blade blurted.

"You mean perfume, the smelly stuff?" asked One Finger Jimmy.

"That's what I said: poyf-yoom, and she wants it legitimate. That means all paid for and in a little fancy bag with a ribbon."

"You mean we got to enter the store during opening hours?" gasped Chainsaw.

"And we got to talk to the dame on the smelly counter?" added Half-smile Gabrianni. "The one that wears six layers of face paint?"

"How come Dolly don't just want a grenade or a sledgehammer or a bazooka cannon like other folks?" asked Porky.

"Because Dolly is a genteel and refined member of the weaker sex," said Blade. "And if she don't get what she wants then she's likely to burst in here and rip us to bits, chew us up, spit us out and stamp her heels into the quivering pieces."

"Well I don't want to be seen at no smelly counter buying no little bag of perfume from no paint-face lady," said Weasel. "Boy, I'd be laughed out of town."

"There is a way," said Blade. "When the coast is clear, we send in two bagmen."

"Why two?" said Numbers.

"It cuts the time," said Blade. "While one is getting the smelly all wrapped up nice and pretty, the other is already paying the money. Then outside we need a driver waiting to get them away from Goldtopps and *fast*."

"But suppose it takes a long time choosing the ribbon?" said Porky.

"Or maybe the paper won't fold or they've lost the scissors or something?" said Jimmy. "I sure wouldn't like to be hanging round there if Bluetooth Fonetti or one of the East side boys walked in."

"We need lookouts," said Blade. "Here's the plan. We need to position men so that every road, street and alley on this map is covered. That way if anybody approaches the store, we can blow the whistle and scram."

"But look at it!" moaned Weasel. "It'll take dozens of men to watch everything!"

As ever, Weasel was wrong, but can you work out what is the smallest number of lookouts needed to be able see down every street on the map – and where should they stand?

Cross and Even Crosser

Draw a cross shape made of five equal squares and cut it out.

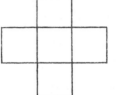

Can you cut the cross into four pieces which are exactly the same size and shape? There are at least *three* different ways to do this!

You have to cut the cross into four pieces which are exactly the same, but then you have to be able to put the pieces together to make *two squares* which are the same size!

And if you think you're SO clever – this cross puzzle will make you even crosser...

Draw *two* equal cross shapes and cut them out. Cut each shape into two pieces with one straight cut. Assemble the four pieces to make *one big square*!

 Get a calculator and work out 1 ÷ 9.

Pass the Poison

Thag the Mathemagician came across this gruesome scene in the barbarians' games room! "What diabolical game has been played here?" he muttered.

Then he noticed a scroll with instructions nailed to the wall with a goat's tooth:

PASS THE POISON!

A game for nine incredibly stupid players

- All nine players shall sit around the table.
- One player starts the game by taking the poison bottle and passing it to the left.
- The seventh living person who touches the bottle must drink from it.
- The next person picks the bottle from the hands of the new corpse, and the bottle is passed around again.
- Again, the seventh living person who touches the bottle must drink from it.
- Play continues until everyone is dead.

"Interesting!" mused Thag. "Obviously the eighth person to drink from the bottle finished it, so Mungoid survived and could leave the table. This raises two questions. Who started the game and who finished the poison?"

PAGE 10

The Megavolt Vaults

HAR HAR! WELCOME TO MY VAN DER GRAAF ELECTRICAL VAULTS!

All the floors are made of rubber, so you won't get a shock as you pass through – but the bad news is that you'll be charged up with millions of volts as you go!

You have to find your way through the rooms to the exit.

- You start off with *zero* charge.
- You must pass through even - and odd-numbered rooms alternately.
- For every *even*-numbered room you pass though you must *add* that number of megavolts to your charge.
- For every *odd*-numbered room you must *take away* that number of megavolts from your charge.

Mystery Tour

SCORE UPDATE: Add 7 points.

NEXT CLUE:

My first is in sea and also in shore,
My second is so I can see all the more,
My third can be cross or times by a lot,
My fourth is quite often poured out of a pot,
My fifth is a question all in a letter,
My next escapes lock but its caught up in fetter,
All the rest describes mine and yours.
But that's not the end of this riddle, because...
The number you seek can be caught unawares as
A pair of pairs of pairs of pairs of pairs of PAIRS.

- You must not let your voltage go negative. (So obviously you must start by stepping into room number 8.)
- When you step outside, your voltage must be exactly zero. Otherwise when you make contact with the earth you will frazzle!

The Darts of Doom!

CLUNK! The door swings shut behind you. On the wall you can see a target.

"I challenge you to darts," snortles the Professor. "I'm brilliant at this! The only way you're allowed out is if you beat me!"

"Humph," you say casually.

"And we play to *my* rules!" laughs the Professor. "We pick a number for each other, and the first player to score that total with three darts is the winner! And guess what number I'll pick for you? Yes – 150!"

"Then I'll pick 151 for you!" you reply.

"Oh no you don't!" says the Professor. "The highest score you can get with three darts is 150, so you've got to pick a smaller number for me than that."

Goodness! The only way to beat him is to hit all three darts in the bullseye before he gets whatever number you pick for him. However it turns out that you *can* beat the Professor – because there are some numbers that are impossible to score with three darts!

What is the *lowest* impossible score you could ask the Professor to get with three darts? (Darts that miss count as zero points.)

The Professor changes the rules so that ALL three darts must score and must be in different sections of the board. What is the highest *possible* score you could get? And you won't be able to score 0, 1, 2, 3, 4 or 5, but what is the next lowest *impossible* score?

30

The Cross Sums

When it's tea-break time in the Murderous Maths testing laboratory, all the utterly nutty Pure Mathematicians like to gather round and do the cross sum. It's just like a crossword puzzle, but instead of filling in letters, you have to fill in numbers. Here's how it works:

If there's a sum with a gap like this: $9 - \square = 6$ then obviously the number to go in the box would be a "3".

Here's today's cross sum, so see if you can beat the Pure Mathematicians by filling all the missing numbers into the grid.

THERE ARE NO NUMBERS BIGGER THAN 9.

CAN YOU WORK OUT WHAT GOES IN THE TOP RIGHT-HAND CORNER?

IF YOU WANT TO BE AS BRAINY AS US, TRY WORKING IT OUT IN YOUR HEAD WITHOUT WRITING ANYTHING DOWN!

Mystery Tour ⟨?⟩

SCORE UPDATE: Add 1 point.
NEXT CLUE: What two-digit number gives the same answer whether you divide it by 2 or just add the two digits together?

By the way – if you get lost on the mystery tour, the correct page order is in the 'Drastic Answers' section.

Master Fiendish's Homework

Of course, I wasn't always a brilliantly diabolical professor. No, it took years of dedicated training and much of my inspiration came from my maths teacher, Miss Tayke. Here are a few of the homework sums she set us – see if you could answer them!

1 What is one-half of two-thirds of three-quarters of four-fifths of five? (This should take you about one second to work out!)

2 In two hours it will be half the time to midnight as it will be from midnight. What time is it now?

3 A hat and a scarf costs £12. A coat and an umbrella costs £17. A coat and a hat costs £24. What does an umbrella and a scarf cost?

4 If a "dozen" means 12, which of these two is bigger: half a dozen dozen, or six dozen?

5 If 3 men can dig 2 holes in 6 hours and 2 men can dig 6 holes in 1 hour and 11 men can dig 1 hole in 12 hours, how many holes can 4 men dig in 4 hours?

6 In the old days there used to be 12 old pennies to one shilling and 20 shillings to £1. If I bought a brand-new posh house for £3/11/4 (which means 3 pounds 11 shillings and 4 pence) how much change would I have from a £5 note?

HE USED TO BE THE TEACHER'S PET. SHE KEPT HIM IN A CAGE ON THE WINDOWSILL.

TOYS

Ready to Rock!

I've booked the Girlie Boys to play in my basement. They are the loudest band in town so it should annoy my neighbours perfectly. All I need to do is plug each guitar into its matching amplifier. Also, each amplifier needs to be plugged into the wall sockets at the back.

Of course the Girlie Boys play SO LOUD that there are trillions of megavolts passing down all the wires. As I don't want massive blue zaps destroying my underground mansion, can you see how to link everything up correctly so that no wires have to cross each other? (The wires can be made as long as you like, but they must not run in front of the band – I don't want them tripping up and frying themselves.)

 Imagine a third line drawn between A and C.

The Card Square

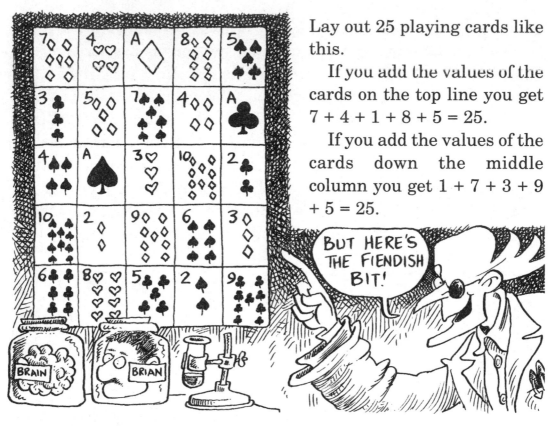

Lay out 25 playing cards like this.

If you add the values of the cards on the top line you get 7 + 4 + 1 + 8 + 5 = 25.

If you add the values of the cards down the middle column you get 1 + 7 + 3 + 9 + 5 = 25.

Can you rearrange the cards so that:
- every column adds to 25
- every row adds to 25
- … and all four corners plus the centre card add to 25?

The Fiendish Family Portrait

Uncle Cain Fiendish was 40 years old when Drusilla was born.
Granny Malsquot Fiendish was 20 years older than Uncle Cain.
Bagpipe Fiendish was born 30 years before Drusilla.
In the picture Drusilla is half as old as Granny.
How old is Bagpipe Fiendish in the picture?

PAGE 21

Mystery Tour

Hello! This should be your first stop on the Mystery Tour.

SCORE UPDATE: Start your score with 20 points.

NEXT CLUE: Each number in the grid should be made by multiplying the number on the top by the number on the side (e.g. 56 = 7 × 8), but some of them are wrong! If you coloured in the correct numbers, what number would be revealed?

	2	6	7	4	5
9	18	54	63	28	45
3	6	21	17	14	15
4	8	24	28	12	20
8	18	52	56	48	40
7	14	42	49	32	35

SwingalongaTitus

LADIES AND GENTLEMEN, WILL YOU PLEASE WELCOME THE WORLD'S MOST TALENTED, POPULAR AND GOOD-LOOKING ENTERTAINER, **MR TITUS O'SKINTY!**

Titus has got four massive hits from his recent demo tape he'd like to share with you:

- "Yes I'm adorable" and "Kiss my shoes" together last exactly 12 minutes.
- "You love me too much" and "Yes I'm adorable" together last exactly 11 minutes.
- "Kiss my shoes" and "Devoted to me" together last exactly 8 minutes.

How long would it take to perform all four songs?

If "You love me too much" lasts 4 minutes, how long is "Devoted to me"?

Mystery Tour

SCORE UPDATE: Subtract 120 points.

NEXT CLUE: If you wait from quarter past one to twenty to three, how many minutes is that?

The Miser Isles

Do you have fabulous dreams of scuba diving, sunbathing, lip-smacking food, parties, skiing, games and swimming pools? If so, then I recommend a holiday on the Miser Isles. That's because they've got big beds there and you can lie in them and dream as much as you like about anything you fancy. However, if you are brave enough to leave your room, watch out for the islanders!

Their currency is the Fleess and they only have two different coins. One of their favourite tricks is when the bus comes along and you're supposed to have the correct money ready, because they won't give you change! If the fare is 11F then the best you can do is hand over a 13F coin. You'll end up paying 2F more than you should! But which of these fares is the *most* unfair?

And if you go to the Olde Gifte Shoppe and want to buy three different items, which should you choose if you want to spend as little as possible, but be able to give the exact money?

And finally, when you go to the "Restaurant of 1,000 Tips" which of these dishes is the only one that you can't give the exact change for?

MENU	
SQUID IN MARMALADE 62F	FUNGI ROULETTE 54F
DEEP-FRIED BLACK FOREST GATEAU 69F	BEE STEW 85F
	HORSETAIL PIE 71F

The Sauce-O-Matic

Why not, I thought? I'll try anything once, and so I invented a device to help kids and mums with that old problem – unscrewing the top off the sauce bottle! Here's the result. Natty, eh?

You can see the bottle is firmly clamped on to the lower wheel and the top is help tight by the grips under the upper wheel. All you need to do is turn the handle as indicated and in seconds the bottle will opened. Quick, convenient and ... well, expensive – but I've got to have *some* reward for my efforts, haven't I?

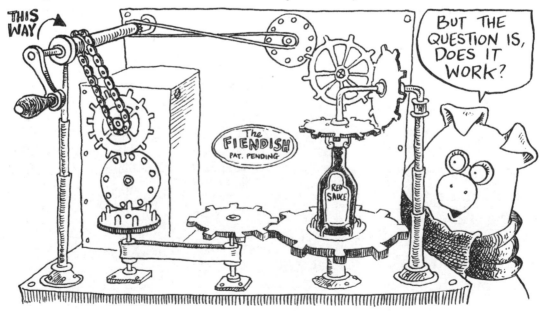

The Footskull League

The sands of the Forgotten Desert have been the stage for many ghastly events, but possibly none of them were quite so breakfast-reappearing as the Footskull League. It's very similar to football, there are just two differences. One is that the offside rule doesn't apply if the captain of the offending team is holding a triple-bladed axe over the referee, and the other is that it isn't a ball that gets kicked around. That's why it isn't called football.

The rules of the league table are that:

A **WIN** SCORES **3** POINTS

A **DRAW** SCORES **1** POINT

A **LOSS** SCORES **0** POINTS

Last year, three teams played: Urgum the Axeman's Seventeen Sons, Grizelda the Grisly's Amazon Army and Colonel Cancel's Valiant Vector Warriors.

Each team played each other once, and these were the results: Urgum beat Grizelda, Grizelda beat the Colonel, and the Colonel drew with Urgum.

Can you work out what points each team finished with on the league table?

This year, Hunjah the Headless and his Spectral Allstars joined the league and here are the final points: Grizelda 7, Hunjah 4, Urgum 3 and Colonel 2. Can you work out the results of the six matches?

URGUM v GRIZELDA
COLONEL v URGUM

GRIZELDA v HUNJAH
URGUM v HUNJAH

HUNJAH v COLONEL
COLONEL v GRIZELDA

SHOVE!

SPLAT!

TRIP!

SPLURK!

GLITCH!

PAGE 45

Bury the Ace!

"Forget it, Lil!" snapped Brett Shuffler. "I'm not playing! Every time I come into the Last Chance Saloon, you always cheat me out of my money."

"Don't you be sore with me, Brett!" said Riverboat Lil. "Besides, this game only uses my money. We don't even need to see yours!" So saying, Lil tipped a small velvet bag of pennies on to the table.

"I'm still not interested," said Brett, not realizing that he'd already pulled up a chair, and sat down. "You'll be using a trick pack of cards or something!"

"Just the one card," said Lil. "And no trick – it's just a nice plain normal ace of diamonds. Now you hush your mouth while I explain the rules of this quaint little parlour sport..."

The game is simple enough for any two people to play. All you need is an ace from a pack of cards and *loads* of coins. They can all be the same, or they can be a mixture providing you've got lots of each sort.

- Lie the ace face up on a table.
- The first player puts a coin anywhere on the card.
- The second player adds another coin anywhere, so long as it lies flat on the card without overlapping the first.
- The first player then adds another coin ... and so on.
- You're not allowed to move any coins that are already in position.
- The loser is the first person who cannot fit a coin completely on to the ace without it overlapping the edge!

Back in the Last Chance Saloon, Brett and Lil played right through until sun up. The amazing thing was that when Brett placed the first coin, sometimes he won and sometimes Lil won. But when Lil placed the first coin she *always* won!

So what was Lil's sneaky secret?

Devious Quickies: 1) $56 = 7 \times 8$; **2)** Pages 19, 20, 23, 37, 38 and 42 will also be missing; **3)** $98 - 76 + 54 + 3 + 21 = 100$; **4)** The battery costs 50p. (The CD player costs £100.50 and so £100.50 + 50p = £101); **5)** The train was 8 hours and 1 minute late. The next time the digits add to 22 is 17:59, so that's when the train expected at 09:58 arrived; **6)** $32 \times 3125 = 100,000$; **7)** 3 miles. (Pongo rode $7134 - 7112 = 22$ miles. 14 miles was his first trip to Aunt Aroma's leaving 8 miles to the puddle and back. This makes the puddle 4 miles from his house; so it's 3 miles from Aunt Aroma's.); **8)** 11,012,111; **9)** 3 boys and 4 girls; **10)** b; **11)** It has all the digits from 0 to 9 in it!; **12)** 8008 41414 100001.

The Romantic Roses: The Prof only delivered four roses! Two short-stemmed red and two long-stemmed white!

Ten Tantalizing Cards: Here's one solution for the cards and one for the dominoes:

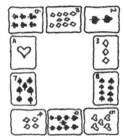 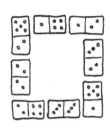

Calculator Hunting: $11 \div 13$, $13 \div 17$, $17 \div 22$, $22 \div 23$, $23 \div 26$, $26 \div 29$

$7 + 7 - 9 = 5$ $8 + 8 + 9 = 25$ $7 \times 7 + 9 - 8 = 50$ $99 + 8 - 7 = 100$

The Meter Cheater: Smallest is the station, most is the hospital. Total collected = £320 (station = £40, school = £60, petrol = £100, hospital = £120)

The Serpent Stones: It *can* be done ... just make sure you step on the square stone once.

The Nasty Sur-prizes: You can't score 27 points on either game!

The Security Grid: Cash point 1259, passport 2023, post office account 534928, bicycle padlock 1962, fridge safe 66949, shed 027.

Bolt Cutters: The longest possible chains are: **a)** 4 4 4 4; **b)** 6 6 6 12; **c)** 8 8 12; **d)** 8 16 4; **e)** 4 5 6 7 8; and 11 unused intact links (not including the unused link in the first example).

The Ravenous Rajah: 3! To eat 3 curries, you'll need $4\frac{1}{2}$ ice creams, but you can't buy $\frac{1}{2}$ portions, so you need to buy 5 ice creams. So far you've spent $3 \times £1.40 = £4.20$ on the curries and $5 \times 70p = £3.50$ on ice cream, making £7.70 altogether. Out of your £12 this leaves £4.30 for drinks. As you need 3 drinks for every ice cream you eat, you might think you need $5 \times 3 = 15$ drinks which would cost £4.50 and that's too much!

But although you are buying 5 ice creams you only need to eat $4\frac{1}{2}$ of them, so you only need $4\frac{1}{2} \times 3 = 13\frac{1}{2}$ drinks. As 14 drinks will cost £4.20 you *can* afford them. Your total bill will be £4.20 + £3.50 + £4.20 = £11.90, so you can even leave Kumar a 10p tip!

Pongo's Deluxe Burger Bar: Nobody had the diced carrots. £1.73 = blue pop, pan scrapings, sprouts; £1.90 = chewy soup, pan scrapings, chips; £2.27 = chewy soup, curry, sprouts; £1.99 = coffee and tea mix, curry, chips; £1.56 = blue pop, eggy cheese, chips.

The Laboratory Shelf: 1 = Fox Scent, 2 = Frog Spawn, 3 = Pig Dribble, 4 = Ant Blood, 5 = Otter Sweat, 6 = Worm Juice.

Charity Day: From the dustbin, go East then South, paying £1. Keep going S past the little square, then W then S paying £2. Keep going S, but over to the W side paying another £1. Then cut through E, but just before you reach the £3 collector, go N then E paying £1. Then make your way N then E paying £1 and then paying £2. Come S, but go round the block avoiding the next £2 collector. Then go E and S, pay £1, then go the long way round the block below you, finally pay £1 and then go S for the sandwich.

The Stake Out: Only three lookouts are needed.

Cross and Even Crosser:

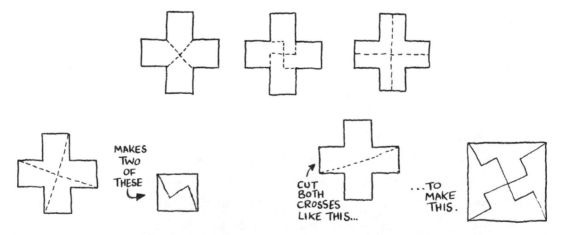

Pass the Poison: Deltar started the game and Deltar also finished the poison. (When Deltar started the game he was the first person to touch the bottle.) The order that the players drank the poison is Junj, Shottran, Krunz, Gorgo, Ffarg, Rediff, Xanto, Deltar.

The Megavolt Vaults: +8 − 5 + 12 − 7 + 14 − 9 + 6 − 13 + 4 − 3 + 4 − 11 = 0.

The Darts of Doom: Lowest impossible score = 81. With new rules the highest possible = 88, and lowest impossible = 49.

The Cross Sums: The number in the corner is 6 … you work out all the others yourself!

Master Fiendish's Homework: 1) 1. It's $\frac{1}{2} \times \frac{2}{3} \times \frac{3}{4} \times \frac{4}{5} \times 5$ which cancels to become $\frac{1}{5} \times 5 = 1$; **2)** 2:00 p.m. (or 14:00 hrs). In two hours it will be 4:00 p.m. which is 8 hours to midnight and 16 hours from midnight; **3)** £5. You can easily see that a hat + scarf + coat + umbrella costs £12 + £17 = £29. Therefore as the coat and hat costs £24, that leaves £5 for the umbrella and scarf; **4)** They both equal 72; **5)** As many as you like. All the holes in the question are different sizes – it depends what size you want!; **6)** £1/8/8 which was enough to buy a new car.

Ready to Rock:

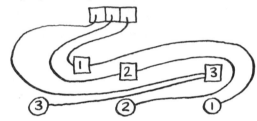

The Card Square: Swap over the two black aces with the two sixes!

The Fiendish Family Portrait: Bagpipe is 90 in the picture. (Granny is 120, Drusilla is 60 and Uncle Cain is 100.)

SingalongaTitus: All four songs take 19 minutes, "Devoted to me" takes 3 minutes.

The Miser Isles: Brownpool Beach – you'll pay 4F too much! In the shop buy a jigsaw, a toilet roll holder and a nit comb costing 67F (pay with $3 \times 13F$ and $4 \times 7F$). You can't pay exactly 71F for Horsetail Pie.

The Sauce-O-Matic: No! If you turn the handle as shown, the top will be screwed on tighter!

The Footskull League: Last year: Urgum 4, Grizelda 3, Colonel 1. This year: G beat U; G beat H; G drew with C; H beat U; H drew with C; U beat C.

Bury the Ace: You can also win if you know Lil's secret! When Lil places the first coin, she puts it exactly in the middle of the card. (That's why she used an ace of diamonds – it's the easiest card to tell where the exact centre is.) Then every time Brett puts down a coin, Lil copies the same move exactly on the opposite side of the centre coin. That way, as long as Brett can find a place for a coin, so can Lil!

The DRASTIC Brainbenders

OH — SO YOU THINK YOU'VE FINISHED THE EASY SECTION, DO YOU? WELL, HERE'S A QUICK IDEA OF HOW BRAINY YOU'LL NEED TO BE FOR THE NEXT LOT...

1 Here are the numbers zero to nine in a special order. Can you tell where the number ten should fit into the line?
8 5 4 9 1 7 6 3 2 0

2 If Blade Boccelli gives One Finger Jimmy $2, then they both have the same amount of money. But if Jimmy gives Blade $3, then Blade will have twice as much money as Jimmy. How much do they each have?

3 The railway journey from Brownpool to Scaggbottom takes 3 hours. Trains leave Brownpool on every hour (e.g. 1:00, 2:00, 3:00...). Trains leave Scaggbottom at half past every hour (e.g. 1:30, 2:30 3:30...). If you go from Brownpool to Scaggbottom, how many trains will pass you coming the other way?

4 Can you arrange eight 8's so that they add up to 1,000? (For example, 88 + 88 + 88 + 8 + 8 = 280, so that's no good!)

5 If the month of June has five complete weekends (i.e. Saturday *and* Sunday), what day of the week will the last day of July be on?

6 There has been a bit of a fight in the Professor's tank of green and yellow bottigrubs. All the yellow bottigrubs only have one eye stalk left, but out of the green bottigrubs, exactly half of them have both eyestalks, while the other half don't have any. If there are 38 bottigrubs in total, how many eyestalks are left?

7 If you reverse the digits in Rodney's age you get Primrose's age. Seven years ago Rodney was four times as old as Primrose. How old are they now?

8 As a reward for saving his daughter's parrot, the Great Rhun of Jepatti offered Prince Gullibul a field covered in golden tiles. Each golden tile measured one square metre. If the field was in the shape of a quadrilateral with sides measuring 30 m, 120 m, 20 m and 70 m, how many golden tiles did Prince Gullibul receive?

9 Thag the Mathemagician seems to be able to travel through time:

TWO DAYS AGO I WAS 114 YEARS OLD, BUT NEXT YEAR I'LL HAVE MY 117TH BIRTHDAY.

How does he do it?

10 You are trying to escape from Urgum the Axeman's Castle! There are two doors – one is the safe exit and the other drops you into a pit of steaming-hot poison with snakes in it. Two of Urgum's sons are on guard and you know that one of them is always a liar and the other always tells the truth. You don't know which son is which. What do you need to ask to find out which door to go through?

FIBBER! LIAR!

 First work out how many matches each team must have drawn!

45

Upsetting the Good Ladies

I had planned a bit of fun at the Fogsworth Manor afternoon tea party. I knew that the Duchess had baked six little cakes and each cake was decorated with four little sweets!

Aha! You've noticed that there are actually seven cakes on the plate, haven't you? That's because I put my own cooking skills to the test. Did you know that if you mince up lots of worms and slugs and boil them up with washing powder, you end up with a yellowy gunge that looks and feels exactly like sponge cake? So I made an *extra* little cake which I slipped on to the Duchess's plate, and arranged the four sweets so that it looked different from the others. Well, I didn't want to eat it by accident, did I? Each of the real cakes has a matching partner, so the first question is: which cake did I make?

Unfortunately, tragedy struck. Rodney Bounder was practising a new overarm shot with his croquet mallet and the ball knocked the cake plate flying. The Duchess quickly scooped the cakes back up and picked all the grass, leaves and dead insects off them. Then, just as she was plonking them back on the plate...

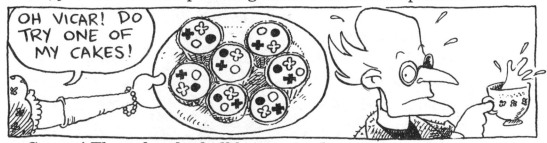

Curses! The cakes had all been mixed up and turned around, so which of them could I be SURE were safe?

How many patterns can you make with four sweets on a cake so that each cake *always* looks different from the others, no matter how they are turned round?

Meanwhile on the patio, Primrose Poppett was threading large coloured beads on to strings to make three bracelets…

At first you might think it's obvious which bracelet has the stink bombs, but the trouble with bracelets is that they can be flipped over as well as rotated. If you just have three coloured beads on a bracelet, there is only one pattern you can make!

How many different patterns could you make using four different beads on each bracelet? How many different patterns using five or six different beads?

Primrose started putting *four* beads on to each bracelet, and she made several in two different patterns. This time the professor managed to add an extra bracelet which does have a different pattern to all the others.

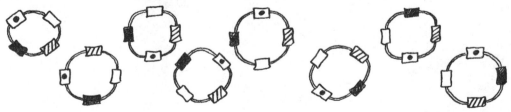

Can you spot it?

The Fiendo

This is surely the Professor's most diabolical plot *ever*! He's planning to replace all the different sorts of money in the world with his own special money "to make things simpler", so he says! If you suspect there might be a catch in it, then you might just be right. . .

There are three sorts of coins:

FIENDOS   **MOTLEYS**   **PROFS**

They work like this:

- One Motley and one Fiendo is worth five Profs.
- Two Profs and one Motley is worth one Fiendo.
- One Fiendo on its own is worth £20.

You check your pocket and find you have four Motleys and one Prof. What's that worth in pounds?

PAGE 13

The Murderous Maths Organization

With any other firm the most important person would be the President (even though they don't tend to do much) and then a Chief Executive, then a Managing Director and so on. But at MM towers fancy titles don't mean a thing – it's your actual job that really matters!

Importance is measured by a number from 8 down to 1, with the most important person being number 8 and the most grovelly person being number 1.

- The Telephone Answerer is four places more important than the One who can Spell.
- The Guardian of the Stapler is two places less important than the Holder of the Door Key.
- The Convenience Hygienist is three places more important than the Light Bulb Changer.
- The Understander of the Photocopier is one place less important than the Waterer of the Rubber Plant.
- The Telephone Answerer isn't as important as the Holder of the Door Key.

Can you put everybody in their order of importance – and so work out who's in charge?

PAGE 84

Unlucky Dip!

Here are five nice cute little presents I've wrapped up for the lucky dip at the village fair. I've been a good boy too, because four of them actually contain something nice, but one of them contains a pickled bottigrub from my slime cabinet!

The four nice presents are absolutely identical to each other, no matter how you turn them over – but the fifth is different! Can you tell which present contains the bottigrub?

TO HELP YOU, THE FOUR NICE PRESENTS CAN ALL BE MADE BY FOLDING THIS NET INTO A CUBE, BUT THE NASTY PRESENT CAN'T!

YOU COULD ALSO TRY MAKING A CUBE OUT OF BLU-TAC AND THEN MARKING THE ARROWS WITH A PENCIL POINT.

SCRIBBLE

Bah! I see that wretched ham joint has been helping you again. Well here are five *more* presents – four nice and one nasty! See if you can work out which one contains the mouldy bellimite. Oh and this time – no help!

Mystery Tour

SCORE UPDATE: Add 17 points.

NEXT CLUE: 79 is a prime number because it doesn't divide exactly by anything except 1 and itself. What is the closest prime number to it?

The Three Coin Conundrums

Conundrum 1 (slightly diabolical)

Arrange any eight coins in a row:

You have to end up with four piles of two coins:

- You move the coins one at a time.
- You only have four moves.
- Each coin must pass over exactly two other coins, no more and no less! (Remember that two coins in a pile count as two coins!)

Conundrum 2 (a bit diabolicaller)

Arrange four copper and four silver coins in a row like this:

You have to end up with this:

- You must move two coins each time.
- They must be touching.
- You can't swap them over while you're moving them.

 THIS IS NAUGHTY

- You have a maximum of *four* moves!

Conundrum 3 (beastly diabolical)

Arrange three copper and two silver coins like this:

The challenge is to move them so they end up like this:

- This time you are allowed *five* moves.
- The rules are the same as last time except that each time you move two coins, it *must* be one copper and one silver.
- Remember you musn't swap them over while you're moving them!

Mystery Tour

SCORE UPDATE: Add 29 points.

NEXT CLUE: If I have less than £1 in coins, what is the largest amount of money I could have and not be able to give someone exactly 50p? (For example, you could have three 20p coins and one 5p coin. Even though that makes 65p in total, you could still not give exactly 50p! But the answer to this question is higher than 65p.)

Win a Warthog with Titus O'Skinty!

It's show time, folks, and once again Titus is proudly pushing back the frontiers of taste by giving away – yes, *giving* away – some furry friends to the winners of his great new TV game.

The show features a cage full of warthogs, which are the prizes. In another cage are the contestants. To save confusion, the warthog cage has a sign saying "warthogs" on it.

Alphonse, who was delighted to be voted the ugliest contestant by the studio audience, won half the warthogs plus half a warthog.

Fifi was disappointed to only be the second ugliest contestant, but she won half the warthogs left for having the most fantastic combination of screeching laugh and painful hair style.

After Fifi got her prize, Lulabelle got the consolation prize for being the rudest contestant, so she won half the warthogs left plus half a warthog.

And finally there was only one warthog left, so that went to Dwight because he amused everyone by smelling so awful.

It really was a great piece of television – did you see it? In case you didn't and you are worried – all the warthogs trotted out of the studio in a fit and healthy state.

So how many warthogs were in the cage to start with?

The Line-Up

City: **Chicago, Illinois, U.S.A.**
Place: **The 8th precinct jail house**
Date: **3 June 1928**
Time: **3:15 p.m.**

"Nothing to say, huh?" sneered Lieutenant Ptchowsky. "Six of your gang were seen getting away from Goldtopps real fast."

BLADE   WEASEL   ONE FINGER JIMMY   CHAINSAW CHARLIE   NUMBERS   HALF-SMILE   PORKY

"But Lieutenant!" gasped Blade. "We ain't done nothing suspicious!"

"That's exactly *why* I'm suspicious," replied Lieutenant Ptchowsky. "So let's find out who did what."

He checked his notes:

The job had involved three lookouts, two bagmen and one driver.

In the line up, the two bagmen were standing together, but none of the lookouts were next to each other.

The driver was standing somewhere between Weasel and Half-smile.

Numbers can't drive and Porky was not a lookout.

Two of the lookouts only had the driver between them.

So which man was not involved at all?

 The clocks were set as the church chimed the hour and Rodney's is broken – so which one is his?

55

Hands in the Dark

A chilly wind was heard whistling down from Fogsworth Manor as everyone gathered for the Duchess's seance. While Croak the butler pulled the heavy curtains across the window, the 13 guests slowly filed into the drawing room. A single candle was burning in the middle of the large circular table around which were placed 13 seats. No one hurried to sit down because although none of them cared about which seat they took, they were all quite fussy about whose hands they are going to be holding in the dark.

"Oh for goodness' sake!" said the Duchess plonking herself onto a chair. "Let's get on with it. I'll sit here and Colonel, you come and sit to my left. Then you choose who you want."

From the 11 people still standing he picked Primrose Poppet and then Primrose picked old Auntie Crystal and so on. The last person to sit down was Binky Smallbrains who ended up on the Duchess's right and finally everyone was happy with the two people they were sitting between. Croak switched off the main lights, which just left the candle burning. In the flickering gloom everyone reached out to hold hands in a big circle.

"ARGHH!" Primrose screamed and Croak hurriedly snapped the lights back on.

Primrose had not realized that the secret of Auntie Crystal's fantastic harpsicord playing was that she had seven fingers on her right hand.

"Do you mind if I hold your other hand, Auntie?" asked Primrose.

"I'll have to cross my arms," said Auntie Crystal.

"Oh no you don't!" said the Duchess. "That would confuse the spirits. We'll have to think of something else.

"I say," said Binky. "What if we all turn our chairs round and face away from the table? Then we'll be next to the same two people, but holding each other's other hand."

"Hopeless!" said the Duchess. "If we're all facing away then how will we see the candle float up into the air? After all, that's why we're here."

"Got it!" said the Colonel. "We all turn ourselves over and sit upside down on our heads. That way we can use our other hands and still see everything."

"Colonel!" snapped the Duchess. "Some of us are wearing skirts and I for one am not prepared to let you see everything."

"Ahem," coughed Croak from the doorway.

"Speak up, Croak," said the Duchess.

"If I might suggest…" began Croak.

What was Croak's solution?

 There are no tricky sums here! Just think how long it took before the two spaceships collided!"

The End of the Tour!

IF YOU'VE BEEN DOING THE MYSTERY TOUR THEN WELL DONE — YOU'VE REACHED THE END!

It's time for the very last adjustment to your score:

Mystery Tour

SCORE UPDATE: Multiply by 3.

That's it! You should now have a final total which consists of three digits which are all different. If it doesn't, you've gone wrong somewhere. This final total is going to be your CODE NUMBER to help you read the secret message on the opposite page!

Here's how the code works:

Suppose the message is "I love you". (Don't panic! It isn't that. Yukkk!) Each letter is changed to a two-digit number like this:

a	b	c	d	e	f	g	h	i	j	k	l	m
01	02	03	04	05	06	07	08	09	10	11	12	13

n	o	p	q	r	s	t	u	v	w	x	y	z
14	15	16	17	18	19	20	21	22	23	24	25	26

The message is then written out in numbers (ignore the spaces between words). We'd get...

09   12   15   22   05   25   15   21

Then suppose the code number was 748, you just go along the numbers adding 7 to the first one, 4 to the second one, 8 to the third one, then 7 to the fourth number, 4 to the fifth, and so on. You'd get:

	09	12	15	22	05	25	15	21
+	7	4	8	7	4	8	7	4
=	16	16	23	29	09	33	22	25

And there's your coded message – which is very tough to crack unless you know the code number! To decode it you do the sum in reverse and then turn the numbers back into letters:

	16	16	23	29	09	33	22	25
-	7	4	8	7	4	8	7	4
=	09	12	15	22	05	25	15	21
	I	L	O	V	E	Y	O	U

So have you got your code number ready? Here's your message:

27 07 21 16   06 24 18 07   34 19 23   22 25 21 29

06 07   10   11 07 23 13 23 28   16 11 20 09   15 14

16 17 24 15   17 30 24   08 24 22   15 34

19 22 17 09 20   13 13 03 11 19 14 18 07 03 21

07 10 10 16 14 14 18 09 14 23   11 23   24 10 14

17 23 27 08 07 27 19 23 28   17 03 29 12 21

11 19 17 20 23

The Lie Detector

Lil's Dead Giveaway!

The doors of the Last Chance Saloon swung open.

"Well look-ee here!" called a woman seated at a green baize table. "If it ain't my old buddy Brett Shuffler!"

"Riverboat Lil!" gasped Brett. "I heard that you'd left town."

"And I heard that you had a hundred dollars in that big old wallet of yours," smiled Lil. "So I came back."

"I'm not playing any games with you, Lil," muttered Brett. "Somehow I always come away losing."

"Not this time, Brett!" said Lil. "This time I've got a game you can't lose."

Lil fanned out a pack of playing cards, to show they were a completely normal pack – half red and half black.

"You shuffle up the cards, then pick one," said Lil. "You then bet half your money that it's red."

"Half my money is $50," said Brett.

"Right. So if you pick a red card, I'll give you $50, but if it's black then you give me $50. That's gotta be fair, hasn't it Brett?"

"Maybe," muttered Brett, clutching his wallet tightly, "but I'm still not playing."

"Oh come on Brett, for old times' sake! In fact, I'll tell you what I'll do – I'll fix it so that you *have* to win!"

"How's that?" asked Brett.

Lil took four red cards and three black cards from the pack. She let Brett shuffle the seven cards together then asked him to deal them face down in a row.

"We go along the row turning over the cards one at a time. We play all seven cards and each time you bet half your money that the card will be red," said Lil.

"But there's four red cards and only three black ones!" gasped Brett. "So I'll win more times that you."

"I call this game my Dead Giveaway!" said Lil. "C'mon, stop hugging that wallet and let's play!"

Brett started with $100, so he bet half of it which was $50.

The first card was red, so Lil gave him $50 giving Brett a total of $150.

Brett then bet half of his $150 which was $75.

The second card was also red, so Lil gave him $75 making Brett's total into $225.

Next time Brett bet half of $225 which was $112 (near enough). The third card was black, so he passed over his $112 which left him with $113...

The last four cards were played.

"Well shoot ma boot!" gasped Brett. "I won four times, and you won three, and yet I *still* lost money!"

"I'm so sorry, Brett," said Lil, slipping the cash into her purse. "I guess I've never met anybody as unlucky as you!"

Was Brett unlucky or was this one of Lil's tricks? Brett started with $100, but can you tell how much was he left with?

Write down 100 at the top of a piece of paper, and then get four red and three black cards. Mix the cards then turn them over one at a time, adjusting your score as you go. Remember to work out your running total after each card is played, and then divide the total by 2 to see how much what you have to "bet" next time.

The 13 Moons of Zog

The Gollarks on the planet Zog have developed a way of travelling around their 13 moons. According to them it's a…

Of course, to mere humans it just looks like a set of long plastic tubes which you have to crawl down, but don't tell them that because they can get a bit touchy about it.

Well, when you hear something like that you've got to have a go, haven't you?

Mystery Tour

SCORE UPDATE: Square your score (i.e. multiply it by itself)!
NEXT CLUE: A rectangular floor is exactly covered in square tiles. If there are 78 tiles round the edge, what is the *smallest* number of tiles there could be altogether?

Pets' Corner

- The ones with pointy tails are lethal unless they are hairy, in which case they might be safe.
- The stripey ones are lethal unless they have a pointy tail in which case they might be safe.
- All the spotty ones are safe unless they have eyestalks, in which case they might be lethal!
- The plain ones are lethal unless they are hairy in which case they might be safe
- If you're not sure, and it has eyestalks, then you can be sure it's safe.

Sixteen Sixteen Ways

NUMBERS CAN CREATE MANY CURIOUS AND MAGICAL THINGS. SEE IF YOU CAN CONJURE UP THE MYSTERY SIXTEEN SQUARE.

Look at these ten groups of digits:

3247 5245 5245 3463 4444 1465 1465 2626 5371 5335

You'll notice that each group of four digits adds up to 16. (And, yes, there are two matching pairs!)

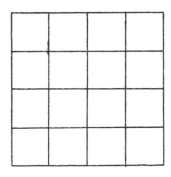

All you have to do is fit all ten groups into this grid so that each group appears once either horizontally, vertically or diagonally, forwards or backwards.

When you've finished you'll have a magic square that has all its horizontal lines adding to 16, all its vertical lines adding to 16 and both diagonals adding to 16, so that makes ten different ways. But here's the magic bit…

* You should also find that all four corners add to 16.
* The four numbers in the middle add to 16.
* And if you split the grid into four quarters, the four numbers in each little square will also add to 16.

That means your square can make a total of 16 in sixteen different ways!

> Start by working out which position the moss eater finished in. (If it finished three places in front of the green rat and five rats are racing, it must be first or second.) However, the slug eater is second, so the moss eater won.

HERE ARE THE ANSWERS TO THE **DRASTIC BRAINBENDERS.**

Drastic Quickies: 1) The 10 should come between the 6 and the 3. It's more obvious to write this as "the TEN should come between the SIX and the THREE" because all the numbers are written out in alphabetical order!; **2)** Blade has $17 and Jimmy has $13; **3)** You'll pass six trains. (If you leave at 3:00, the six trains from Scaggbottom will be the 00:30, 1:30, 2:30, 3:30, 4:30 and 5:30.); **4)** 888 + 88 + 8 + 8 + 8 = 1000; **5)** July 31st will be on a Wednesday; **6)** There are 38 eyestalks left! (It doesn't matter how many bottigrubs are green or yellow.); **7)** Rodney is 31 and Primrose is 13; **8)** The prince received exactly NO golden tiles! (Try drawing the field to find out why!); **9)** Thag's birthday is on December 31st and he's speaking on January 1st. Two days before he was 114, at the time he was speaking he is 115, on his birthday this year he'll be 116 and on his birthday next year he'll be 117; **10)** You say to one of the sons, "Which door would your brother say is safe?" Which ever door he points to, you must go through the other one!

Upsetting the Good Ladies:

This is the Prof's cake:

These cakes are definitely safe:

You can make six different patterns:

Four beads make 3 patterns, five beads make 12 patterns, and six beads make 60 patterns. (If you know about factorials you can work this out with a formula. If you have n beads the number of patterns is $\frac{(n-1)!}{2}$ So for seven beads it's $\frac{(7-1)!}{2} = \frac{6 \times 5 \times 4 \times 3 \times 2}{2} = 6 \times 5 \times 4 \times 3 = 360$ patterns.)

This is the Prof's bracelet (it is the only bracelet where the dot bead is opposite the black bead):

The Fiendo: £40. You need to know a bit about equations to solve this one! You can write the values of the coins like this: M + F = 5P   2P + M = F   and then replace the "F" with £20 to give two equations: (1) M + £20 = 5P and (2) 2P + M = £20. The trick is to realize how to adjust the two equations! Here's one way to do it: You adjust the first equation by subtracting £20 from each side so you get M = 5P – £20. You then subtract 5P from each side and get M – 5P = – £20. Multiply the second equation by 3 to get 6P + 3M = £60. You now ADD the two equations together, keeping the money on one side and the letters on the other. You get: M – 5P +6P + 3M = £60 – £20. When you work it out you get 4M + P = £40.

The Murderous Maths Organization: Order of importance starting with most important: Holder of the Door Key, Convenience Hygienist, Guardian of the Stapler, Telephone Answerer, Light Bulb Changer, Waterer of the Rubber Plant, Understander of the Photocopier, and finaly the leest importunt iz the Won hoo kan Spel.

Unlucky Dip: The bottigrub is e and the bellimite is b. This is the net for the safe boxes:

The Three Coin Conundrums:

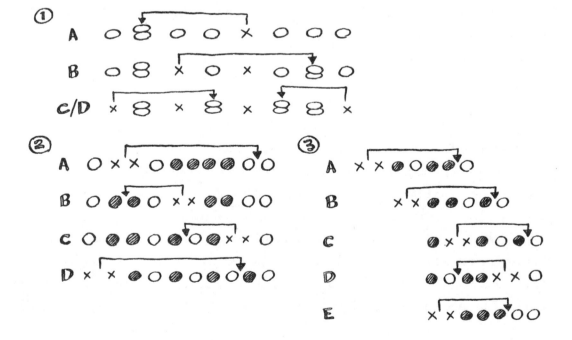

Now that you know the answers to the coin Conundrums, why not see if you can do the tricks backwards? If you get really good at them you can even challenge your friends.

Win a Warthog with Titus O'Skinty: There were 13 warthogs to start with! Alphonse won $6\frac{1}{2} + \frac{1}{2} = 7$ leaving 6 in the cage. Fifi won 3 leaving 3 in the cage. Lulabelle won $1\frac{1}{2} + \frac{1}{2} = 2$ leaving 1 in the cage, which Dwight won.

The Line-Up: Weasel was not involved. (Lookouts: Blade, Jimmy and Numbers. Bagmen: Half-smile and Porky. Driver: Charlie.)

Hands in the Dark: Croak said: "If you all move across the table, the matter would be resolved. You stay where you are, madam, Master Binky and the Colonel swap places, then the two people next to them swap places and then the next two swap, then the next two, then the next two and the final two."

After a lot of climbing over, around and under the table they ended up with Auntie on Primrose's right and Binky on the Duchess's left and so on. Everybody was still sitting between the same two people so once again the lights went out.

"OH YUK!" screamed Primrose.

"Didn't you know my left hand was all thumbs?" chuckled Auntie Crystal.

The End of the Tour: This is the order you should have visited the pages in: 35-51-83-31-18-28-64-78-14-36-85-53-93-12-60-91-58 We're not telling you what the code number is, but we'll give you two clues: the code number does appear somewhere in this book ... and the first letter of the decoded message is "W".

The Lie Detector: 1) LIE! If there were 12 more girls than boys, then either the number of boys and the number of girls are both even, OR the number of boys and the number of girls are both odd. However to get a total of 131 kids, one number has to even and the other has to be odd, so it's impossible. (Unless you have $59\frac{1}{2}$ boys and $71\frac{1}{2}$ girls – but even the Professor's school wasn't that bad!); **2)** TRUE! The bag contains 2 red, 2 grey and 3 yellow socks; **3)** LIE! The only way this is possible is if the Professor is minus 30 years old and his granny is minus 70!; **4)** LIE! If you multiply any even number by any other whole number you always get an even answer. Therefore it doesn't matter how many eggs he bought, if they were 14p each, the total cost must be an even number of pennies. The same with the toadstools, it doesn't matter what they cost, if he bought 22 of them he must have spent an even number of pennies. If you add together two even numbers, you must get an even answer, so his total could not have been £3.17. And he lied again, the omelette was disgusting; **5)** LIE! If four labels are in the right place – the fifth label *has* to go on the remaining jar!; **6)** TRUE! Each side of the square has 8 tiles (not 7!).

Lil's Dead Giveaway: Of course it's a trick! Even though Brett has four winning cards and only three losing cards, he will always end up with just $63.28 out of his $100. It makes no difference what order the cards are turned over. Each time Brett gets a black card, he loses half his money, so he only has half left. This is the same as multiplying his money by $\frac{1}{2}$. So if he has $100 and gets a black card, he ends up with $100 $\times$ $\frac{1}{2}$ = $50. Each time Brett gets a red card, he gets half his money again – so if he starts with $100 he gets $100 $\times$ $1\frac{1}{2}$ = $150. For these sums it's easier to write $1\frac{1}{2}$ as $\frac{3}{2}$. As he bets half his money everytime, we can multiply all the results together. As there are *three* black cards, we multiply by $\frac{1}{2} \times \frac{1}{2} \times \frac{1}{2}$ and as there are *four* red cards we also multiply by $\frac{3}{2} \times \frac{3}{2} \times \frac{3}{2} \times \frac{3}{2}$. To find out what he was left with we work out: $100 \times \frac{3}{2} \times \frac{3}{2} \times \frac{3}{2} \times \frac{3}{2} \times \frac{1}{2} \times \frac{1}{2} \times \frac{1}{2} = 100 \times \frac{81}{128} = 63.28$. Notice that it doesn't matter what order we write the fractions in this sum, and so it doesn't matter what order Brett turns up the seven cards!

The 13 Moons of Zog: It can be done! Start at the right-hand planet base (the one nearest the Gollark). Wherever you go and whatever corners you turn always keep your right hand touching the wall. You won't go down all the tubes, but you WILL visit all the moons and get back.

Pets' Corner: These four are safe:

Sixteen Sixteen Ways:

Here's one solution:

5	6	4	1
3	2	4	7
3	6	4	3
5	2	4	5

The DIABOLICAL Brainbenders

The Secret Angle

Did you know that a square has four equal angles, and they are all 90°? And did you know that if you draw a diagonal across the square, then that splits the corner into two angles of 45°?

If you did, then you might think you're clever, but think about this:

Suppose you have six squares all put together to make a cube, and you draw in two diagonals that meet at the same corner. (Here the diagonals are AB and CB.)

What is the angle between the two diagonals?

Here's the really irritating bit: it's a nice round number that you can work out without any sums or Pythagoras or protractors! (And it *isn't* just 45° + 45° = 90° either!) PAGE 33

The Cannonball Question

Urgum the Axeman has been trying out his new toy – a cannon. Unfortunately, he's a bit short on money and only has one cannonball, so to make sure he doesn't lose it, he fires it straight up in the air.

The ball just manages to brush the underside of a passing vulture cruising at a height of 100 metres before falling to the ground again, where it lands with a crunch on Urgum's foot.

Nice easy question ... can you tell Urgum how far his cannonball travelled in total?

Urgum decides to have another go, but unknown to him, Grizelda the Grisly has crept out from behind a rock and swapped his metal cannonball for a rubber cannonball!

Urgum fires the ball into the air, and then limps hurriedly to one side. Again the cannonball just reaches 100 metres before coming down again, but to Urgum's amazement the ball bounces back up to one-tenth of its previous height. It keeps coming down and bouncing and each bounce is one-tenth of the height of the last one!

Nice hard question ... can you tell Grizelda *exactly* how far in metres the rubber cannonball travelled in total?

Oh, and just a word of advice: Grizelda doesn't understand decimals, so for goodness' sake avoid mentioning them to her!

PAGE 26

The Great Rhun's Spare Room

IN THE GOLDEN PROVINCES MANY THOUSANDS OF YEARS AGO THERE LIVED THE RICHEST MORTAL EVER TO WALK THIS EARTH. HERE IS ONE MORE TALE OF HOW THE ONE KNOWN AS THE GREAT RHUN OF JEPATTI CAME BY HIS WEALTH.

The palace inhabited by the Great Rhun was so large that to get from one end to the other it was necessary to ride on horseback. And wherever the Rhun went, so did his retinue of many minions who also needed to ride on horseback to keep up. Indeed, the retinue was so large that the stables for all their horses were truly massive in their own right – so massive that to get from one end to the other it was necessary to ride on horseback. Thus you will now appreciate, dear listener, how large was the palace in which the Great Rhun dwelt.

And so it was one day that the Grand Cahjoon did approach the Great Rhun, asking if his mother might move into the spare room.

"Indeed she might," replied the Rhun. "But I demand a rent of 10,000 ftarrps per year."

"That is fair and reasonable, oh great one," replied the Cahjoon.

"And the rent shall rise by 400 ftarrps at the end of every year," added the Rhun.

"So in the second year the rent shall be 10,400 ftarrps?" gasped the Cahjoon. "And in the third year 10,800, and in the fourth 11,200?"

"That is so," said the Rhun. "And should she miss payment by as little as one ftarrp, then she will be visited by the Ghinji!"

So saying, the Great Rhun snapped his fingers and the three-tongued mutant leapt to his side and belched a hearty flame.

"Not the Ghinji! Oh pray have mercy, oh great Rhun!" beseeched the Grand Cahjoon. "The amount of money will grow too great! Have I not served you, have I not been loyal? Surely your marvellousness can offer sweeter terms?"

The Great Rhun shrugged.

"I am much touched by your patheticness," declared the Rhun. "And so I offer a different agreement. Instead of 10,000 per year, the rent starts at 5,000 per six months. And this rent rises by 100 ftarrps every six months. Is this better than rising 400 ftarrps every year?"

"Oh Great Rhun, thou art benevolent indeed!" grovelled the Grand Cahjoon, bending to the floor. "Let me kiss your silken slippers in gratitude."

"Very well," said the Rhun, "but don't kiss these ones I'm wearing. They'll get soggy. Go and find some in my cupboard and kiss them."

So the Grand Cahjoon did go to the cupboard of the Great Rhun to lick the footwear therein. And yet as the Cahjoon turned to go, he failed to notice the sly smile of smugness that passed over the face of the Great Rhun of Jepatti.

So had the Great Rhun really offered a better deal?

Breadsticks at Dawn

City: **Chicago, Illinois, U.S.A.**
Place: **Luigi's Diner**
Date: **24 July 1928**
Time: **6:28 a.m.**

"Shhh!" hissed Luigi in excitement. "Get down, they're coming!"

As three heads ducked behind Luigi's counter, the street door creaked open. With a slight squeeze, Porky Boccelli popped through the doorway closely followed by his two brothers, Blade and One Finger Jimmy. The three men headed straight for the centre table without taking their hats off.

"Good morning, gentlemen," said Luigi, standing behind his counter. "You all set to take on the Gabriannis?"

"Sure we're set," drawled Blade Boccelli. "But it seems they overslept. We agreed to meet at six thirty."

"It's a couple of minutes yet," said Luigi, trying to ignore the unlikely selection of people huddled by his knees. If Blade suspected he was going to have an audience, then the hot lead would start flying and Luigi's diner would become Luigi's scrapyard.

Crouched behind the counter were Dolly Snowlips, Lieutenant Ptchowsky, Bluetooth Fonetti and a lot of money.

"So why do they eat breadsticks?" whispered the Lieutenant.

"The Boccelli and Gabrianni families have been feuding for generations," explained Dolly. "But this lot got tired of hospital food so now they have breadstick-eating contests."

"But why so early in the morning?" moaned the Lieutenant.

"They don't want no one to know!" chuckled Dolly. "C'mon, imagine if word got out that the two toughest gangs in town fought by eating breadsticks!"

"And you should see Porky Boccelli munch!" whispered Bluetooth. "He can demolish food by the truckload. It's an emotional thing with him. My money's on the Boccellis."

"Pssst!" Luigi hissed down towards them. "Here come the others."

76

The Gabrianni brothers came in and took their places opposite the Boccellis at the centre table.

"But there's four of them!" said the Lieutenant peering over the counter. "I guess my money's on the Gabriannis!"

"Hmm, I dunno," said Dolly. "Sure there's only three Boccellis, but they do have Porky. Luigi's been taking some notes, so let's check the form. Hey, Luigi!" She tugged Luigi's trouser leg hard.

"Something the matter, Luigi?" enquired Chainsaw Charlie.

"No, no, not at all!" stammered Luigi as he felt a sudden draught shoot up his underpants. Luigi hurriedly pulled his trousers back up and handed down his notepad:

- Blade and Jimmy Boccelli eat at exactly the same speed.
- The four Gabrianni brothers all eat at exactly the same speed.
- Porky and Jimmy together get through breadsticks at exactly the same speed as three of the Gabrianni brothers.
- Porky on his own eats at exactly the same speed as Blade and Jimmy and Half-smile Gabrianni all together.

By now Benni the waiter had put a massive pile of breadsticks in front of the three Boccellis and another equally massive pile in front of the four Gabriannis.

"OK, gentlemen, you know the rules," said Luigi. "The first empty plate wins."

"So where's your money going, Dolly?" asked Bluetooth.

Who should Dolly bet on: the Boccellis, the Gabriannis or could it be a draw?

All Square

If that's too tough, here's something easier to think about…

If you have a square of paper, it's easy to fold it into a square which has a quarter of the area: you just fold it in half and then half again. But how can you fold your paper into a square that has exactly HALF the area?

Mystery Tour

SCORE UPDATE: Add 6 points.

NEXT CLUE: With the number 212, the digits add together to make 5 but multiply together to make 4. What's the smallest number that does this?

The Phazer Bolt

Somewhere out in deep space, an explorer probe manned by the Munts of Yar was spotted by the Evil Gollarks from the planet Zog.

The Gollark spaceship turned and headed directly towards the Munt ship. Thinking the Gollarks were being friendly, the Munts turned and headed straight towards the Gollarks. The Munt ship was moving at 3,000 km per hour and the Gollark ship was moving at 2,000 km per hour.

At the instant the two ships were 5,000 km apart, the Gollarks fired a Phazer Bolt straight at the Munt craft.

Phazer Bolts travel at 134,562,991 km per hour, but the Munts quite sensibly turned on their deflector shield. The Phazer Bolt hit the shield and bounced back towards the Gollarks. Luckily for them, they had a little shaving mirror which they quickly held out in front of them. The bolt then hit the Gollark's mirror and bounced back … and hit the shield and bounced back … and so bounced backwards and forwards between the two spaceships all the time they were closing on each other. Finally, the two ships collided and the Phazer Bolt got trapped between them and disintegrated the lot.

The good news for the Munts is that at the last minute they put on their parachutes and jumped out. The bad news for the Munts is that space has no atmosphere and no gravity, so they are currently floating about wrapped in big floppy sheets.

Just one question then, how far did the Phazer Bolt travel?

PAGE 57

Luigi's Outside Table

Luigi wanted to fix up a table to go outside his diner. As he explained to Benni the waiter: "It's to attract all those fancy folks who like to breathe fumes and have pigeons squat on their plates." So Benni went down to the basement and dragged up an old square table. Luigi figured it was perfect, all it needed was an umbrella to stick up through the middle. That's why he asked Chainsaw Charlie to make a hole for it, but unfortunately Chainsaw didn't quite hit the centre...

And here's the question: how can Charlie chop the tabletop into just *two* pieces and put them together so the hole is exactly in the middle?

 Find the Belgian post-office reserve account number first.

80

The Bottom of the Fridge

I'm treating myself to a cheese and toadstool omelette. Yum!

The different cheeses are all in thumb-size lumps and if you scrape off the green stuff you can see the three different types: blue, yellow and orange.

There's one less blue lump than yellow lumps. There are twice as many orange lumps as blue lumps. If I had two more yellow lumps, they would equal the orange lumps. So how many lumps of cheese have I got?

Once I've moved the cheese aside, I can see my little toadstool garden which grows underneath it.

- All ten of the spotty toadstools are green, and there are also seven plain green toadstools.
- There are 12 poisonous toadstools of which eight are green.
- Seven of the spotty toadstools are poisonous

If all the toadstools are green or poisonous or both, then how many toadstools are there altogether? How many plain green toadstools are safe to eat?

If it was full, my egg box would hold 20 eggs, but it isn't. I want to eat three times as many eggs as I ate yesterday and then that'll leave exactly enough eggs so I can eat half of what I have today tomorrow. As I never eat half eggs, tell me how many eggs I had in the box before yesterday's breakfast.

Coin Pyramids and the End of the World

You need a piece of paper with three crosses on it and a selection of different coins. Put three coins in a pile on one cross, with the

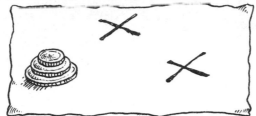

smallest at the top and the largest at the bottom so they form a cute little round pyramid. All you have to do is move the entire pyramid to one of the other crosses BUT...

- You can only move one coin at a time. It can go on a larger coin or an empty cross.
- You may *not* put a larger coin on top of a smaller coin.

What is the smallest number of moves you need to move the entire three coin pyramid to another cross?

Now try the same game with a little pyramid of four coins, then try it with five coins, then six. See what is the smallest number of moves you need for each size of pyramid – and then can you spot the pattern of numbers?

This is a version of a classic old puzzle called The Tower of Hanoi which was based on a legend. There's supposed to be a temple somewhere with a team of monks moving a set of 64 differently sized gold discs following these same rules. Apparently when the last disc is put on top of the new pile, the world will come to an end.

Obviously this sounds like such massive fun that you decide join up with the monks. You dash into the temple to help out, but you're so keen that you trip on your robes and your head crashes into the piles of discs. Let's hope the monks are the silent type, otherwise they'd have a few smart words to say, wouldn't they?

Anyway, they set up the first pile of 64 discs and they start all over again. Remember these discs are massive and solid gold. Suppose it takes one minute to move each disc, it's a diabolical thought but how long have we got until the world ends?

82

Even Crosser Sums

HAR HAR! YOU THINK YOU'VE SEEN ONE OF THESE IN THE **DEVIOUS** SECTION, DON'T YOU?

If you're wondering why another "cross sums" has appeared in the diabolical section … wait until you try it! This one made the Pure Mathematicians even nuttier than they were before!

REMEMBER THAT EACH EMPTY BOX CAN ONLY HOLD ONE DIGIT FROM 0 TO 9.

HAR HAR!

As before, all you have to do is work out what number goes in the top right-hand box – and I bet you can't do this one in you head!

Mystery Tour

SCORE UPDATE: Multiply by 2.

NEXT CLUE: I have five different coins: 1p, 2p, 5p, 10p, and 20p. I can put one or more coins into my piggy bank. How many different totals could I put in the piggy?

The Chauffeur and the Secretary

So, as a matter of personal pride, I'd paid for everything on a credit card. Then, as soon as the bill arrived, I moved to a secret address so the bank couldn't find me and make me pay up. Har har!

Unfortunately, I was just returning to my hideout in the dustbin behind the kebab shop when I noticed a huge gold Rolls Royce parked 100 metres away. It was the bank manager and I had been spotted! Immediately, he sent both his chauffeur and his secretary chasing towards me.

The chauffeur covered 2 metres with every stride, but the secretary (who is shorter) only covered $1\frac{1}{2}$ metres with every stride. I noticed that she could take 4 strides a second, but he could only manage 3 strides per second.

It takes me exactly 15 seconds to unlock the dustbin lid and climb inside, but before I'd done it, one of them grabbed me!

The question is: who got to me first, and how?

 Cut out eight little bits of paper and write the different jobs on each one. Arrange the bits of paper in a line and move them around until they fit all the clues.

The Missing Square

Here's a picture of a nice normal square measuring 10 cm × 10 cm. This means that the area is 10 × 10 = 100 cm².

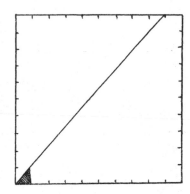

There's a line joining a bottom left corner to a mark 1 cm in from the top right. Apart from that there's nothing suspicious such as levers, wires, trapdoors or mirrors.

BUT NOW WATCH CAREFULLY...

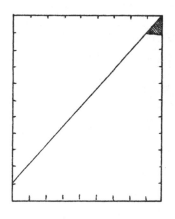

We cut along the line and slide the top bit along slightly.

We then chop off the teeny triangle left at the bottom (coloured black here), and poke it into the little gap that has appeared at the top. It fits exactly, so no problem there. We've just made a normal rectangle.

There's just one little thought to entertain you...

If you count up the marks on the sides, you can see the new rectangle seems to measure 9 × 11 = 99 cm² ... so where's the missing 1 cm² gone?

Mystery Tour

SCORE UPDATE: Divide by 11.

NEXT CLUE: What is the smallest number (apart from 1) that will leave a remainder of 1 when divided by any of 2, 4 or 13?

The Sun and the Pyramid

HERE'S A REALLY TRICKY PUZZLE - YOU CAN TRY IT ON YOUR FRIENDS - IF YOU DON'T LIKE THEM!

You have probably seen a "sliding tiles" game where you have to arrange a picture or a set of numbers by sliding the tiles one at a time into the gap. (You mustn't twizzle the tiles round or simply pick two up and swap them over.) This is the same sort of game – but with a diabolical twist!

This picture shows an equilateral triangle and a little circle which represents the sun rising over the LEFT side of a pyramid.

- Copy this picture *exactly* and then cut out the nine squares.
- Remove the square marked X.
- The object is to slide the tiles around to make the sun appear over the RIGHT side of the pyramid.

So can you make: Look like this:

THIS EGYPTIAN PUZZLE WILL MAKE YOU SPHINX... HAR HAR!

AND THAT JOKE REALLY STINX!

The Tongue Tank

Here's something that came up in the Murderous Maths book "Vicious Circles"…

In the foul city of Fastbuck there was a problem at the Tinned Tongue factory. The factory has a giant circular tank into which they throw all their rejects and bits of off-cut tongues. The trouble is that the tank is full, the waste discharge valve is stuck and to make things worse, a lot of the chopped tongues are still twitching. The handle for the valve is right in the middle of the tank and for some reason nobody has volunteered to wade through the writhing mass of dribble and blood to reach it.

They don't have a ladder long enough to put right across the top of the tank, but they managed to reach the handle by using two ladders of the same length arranged like this:

If the tank is 10 metres across, what is the shortest length of each ladder?

87

Cockroach Café

The Health Inspector found cockroaches running round under the tables but his notes got a bit confused. As he didn't dare walk across the floor, he climbed about from table to table and on each table he wrote down the total number of cockroaches he could see under the *neighbouring* tables.

So if there had only been five tables like this, these are the numbers that he would have written on the tables (and the numbers in the little boxes are the number of bugs UNDER each table). For instance, you'll see that the table with "8" on it touches three other tables which have 2 + 1 + 5 bugs in total underneath.

Here's the table plan for the café with the inspector's numbers written on each table. There is a different number of cockroaches from 0-12 under each table. Which table only has ONE cockroach under it?

COLIN?

MUNCH!

SCRUMP!

PAGE 19

89

The Secret Underground System

Mystery Tour

SCORE UPDATE: Divide by 5.

NEXT CLUE: A car salesman drives a brand-new car for 45,500 miles. He then reverses the connection to the mile meter so that the mileage reading goes *down* rather than up. When he sells the car, the mileage reads 33,000 miles. How many 1,000s of miles should it read?

Crocked Clocks

The landings and stairways of Fogsworth Manor are full of different clocks, and for Croak the Butler, one of his most miserable jobs is setting them all to the right time. He waits for the village church clock to chime the hour, and then he dashes round and puts each clock right. Just for one brief moment they all show the correct time, but sometime later on they look like this:

Each clock has its own little peculiarity:
- Only the Duchess's clock shows the correct time.
- Since being set the Colonel's clock has lost 2 hours and 5 minutes.
- Auntie Crystal has conjured up a rather complex way to double the length of her life – and one of the side effects is that her clock goes at exactly half speed.
- Rodney Bounder's clock hasn't worked ever since the summer when he whacked it with a cricket bat.
- Primrose Poppett's clock gains 10 minutes every hour which is why she's always bright and fresh and early for everything.
- Binky Smallbrain's clock keeps perfect time – it's just that like Binky himself, it goes backwards. (So if you set it to two o'clock, in 90 minutes' time it would show half past twelve.)

So what time is it now?

PAGE 55

The Rat Race

I've built a special track for five rats to race around. It's a bit like a greyhound track, but with one difference. The greyhounds race around following an artificial hare which is being pulled along. My rats race around being followed by a giant cat which is actually me in a costume on my bicycle. All very dignified as I'm sure you'll agree. I've heard the Royal Family enjoy a swanky afternoon at the races, so if Your Majesties are reading this, do invite yourselves round.

The five runners in our last race all had special physical features and each had a favourite food.

- Gungie was not the bald rat that eats pizza boxes.
- The one-eyed rat finished third and Bubonic has no tail.
- The green rat finished three places after the rat that eats moss.
- The spotty rat didn't win.
- Runt isn't bald and has both eyes. He finished two places in front of the cheese-rind eater.
- Scratch eats orange peel and the slug eater came second.

So what position did Scabchops finish in?

BY THE WAY, I'VE GOT A **SIXTH** RAT WHO DOESN'T RACE BECAUSE HE'S TOO BUSY EATING **PORK**!

PAGE 67

Mystery Tour

SCORE UPDATE: Double your points.

NEXT CLUE: You draw three circles and one straight line on a piece of paper so that they all overlap each other. What is the largest number of "crossing points" you can make?

The Secret Angle: 60°. If you draw line AC you'll have made a triangle ABC – and all the sides are equal in length so it's what's called an "equilateral" triangle! Equilateral triangles have all sides equal, and also all the angles are equal to 60° – so the secret angle is 60°.

The Cannonball Question: Urgum's iron cannonball travels 100 m up and 100 m down making 200 m in total. Grizelda's rubber cannonball travels 100 m up and 100 m down, but then goes back up one-tenth of the distance, so that's another 10 m up and down. It then goes back up one-tenth of the distance again so that's another 1 m up and down, then 0.1 m then 0.01 m and so on. In total it travels 222.2222… metres. But unless you write out an infinite numbers of 2's you can't give the answer exactly, and what's more Grizelda doesn't like decimals! However, the hint should have helped you realise that $0.2222 = \frac{2}{9}$ so the exact answer is that Grizelda's cannonball travels $222\frac{2}{9}$ metres.

The Great Rhun's Spare Room: Imagine the rent is paid twice a year. With the first system, the rent is 10,000 for the first year – so that's two payments of 5,000. In the second year the rent is 10,400, which is $2 \times 5,200$ and in the third year it's 10,800, which is $2 \times 5,400$, and so on. With the second system, in the first six months the amount paid = 5,000. But for the second six months the amount paid is 100 more so it's 5,100. For the third six-month period it's 5,200, and so on. Now see what happens over the first four years… With the first system the six-monthly payments would be: $5,000 + 5,000 + 5,200 + 5,200 + 5,400 + 5,400 + 5,600 + 5,600 = 42,400$. The second system for the same period would be: $5,000 + 5,100 + 5,200 + 5,300 + 5,400 + 5,500 + 5,600 + 5,700 = 42,800$. So even though the second system looks like the rent only rises half as fast, in fact the Great Rhun takes an extra 100 every year!

Breadsticks at Dawn: One way to solve this is to make some equations. Let "P" represent Porky, "B" represent the other two Boccelli brothers and "G" represent each of the Gabrianni brothers. Porky and Jimmy Boccelli eat as fast as three Gabriannis, so P + B = 3G. And Porky eats as fast as two Boccellis and one Gabrianni, so P = 2B + G. We are trying to find out if Porky and his two brothers (P + 2B) is more than all four Gabriannis (4B), so we need to work out how many Gs is P equal to, and then how many Gs is 2B equal to. If P + B = 3G, then B = 3G - P. Double this to get: 2B = 6G - 2P.

As P = 2B + G we can swap 2B for 6G - 2P and get P = 6G - 2P + G. This moves around to make 3P = 7G and so P = $\frac{7}{3}$ G or 2 $\frac{1}{3}$ G. As we know P = 2B + G we can swap it round to say 2B = P - G, and now we know that P = 2 $\frac{1}{3}$ G, this tells us that 2B = 2 $\frac{1}{3}$ G - G = 1 $\frac{1}{3}$ G. We can now show that P + 2B = 2 $\frac{1}{3}$ G + 1 $\frac{1}{3}$ G = 3 $\frac{2}{3}$ G. So Porky and his two brothers eat as fast as three and two-thirds of a Gabrianni brother. Therefore four Gabrianni brothers will eat faster!

All Square:

① MARK OFF THE LENGTH OF THE SMALL SQUARE ALONG THE BIG SQUARE TO FIND POINT 'X'.

② JOIN X TO THE TWO CORNERS AND THEN CUT ALONG THE LINES.

③ MOVE THE TWO TRIANGLES ROUND TO MAKE THE SQUARE.

$a^2+b^2=c^2$

OH REALLY?

To fold a square into another square with half the area, just fold the four corners into the middle!

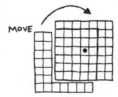

The Phazer Bolt: The Gollarks and Munts are moving together at a combined speed of 2,000 + 3,000 km per hour making 5,000 km per hour. As they were 5,000 km apart when the Phazer Bolt was fired, that means the Phazer Bolt was travelling between them for one hour. As the Phazer bolt travels at 134,562,991 km per hour, it must have travelled 134,562,991 km before the crash.

Luigi's Outside Table: The two pieces are an "L" shape and a rectangle as shown here.

MOVE

The Bottom of the Fridge: 13 lumps of cheese (3 blue, 6 orange and 4 yellow). 21 toadstools; 6 plain green are safe. There were 11 eggs yesterday. (The Prof ate 2 yesterday, he'll eat 6 today and 3 tomorrow.)

Coin Pyramids and the End of the World: For three coins, the minimum number of moves is 7. (The method is to move the smallest coin in the same direction – for example, clockwise – around the three crosses on every alternate turn. On the other turns you move the only other coin that will move to the only place it will move to. It sounds complicated – but try it!) For four coins it's 15, for five coins it's 31 and for six it's 63. There's a simple formula to work it out! If c is the number of coins you're moving, the minimum number of moves is $(2^c - 1)$. So for seven coins it would be $(2^7 - 1) = 128 - 1 = 127$. For the 64 gold discs, the number of moves is $(2^{64} - 1) =$ 18,446,744,073,709,551,615 moves. If you divide this by the number of minutes in a year (which is $60 \times 24 \times 365.25$) you find that the world will end in about 35,072,522,765,437 years. That just about gives you enough time to finish this book.

Even Crosser Sums: The digit in the top right-hand corner is 4. In case you were stuck – first complete the sum on the top line with an "8". (That's easy enough!) When you look at the sum coming down from the 8, the only single digits that will fit in both have to be 9's. The same applies for the sum that starts with the 6 going across the middle. That should be enough to help you complete the grid.

The Chauffeur and the Secretary: The chauffeur managed to reach the Professor in $12\frac{1}{2}$ seconds … because the chauffeur is called Victoria and the secretary is called Albert. (As each stride is 2 m and she takes 4 per second, Victoria can run at $2 \times 4 = 8$ m per second. Therefore she can cover 100 m in $100 \div 8 = 12\frac{1}{2}$ seconds.)

The Missing Square: Actually the finished rectangle measures $9 \times 11\frac{1}{9} = 100$ cm². This is because the line we cut along is not a perfect diagonal of the square, so when the top piece slides along it moves 1 cm to the right but $1\frac{1}{9}$ cm upwards. This enlargement of the little black triangle shows the exact measurements involved.

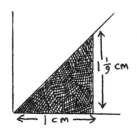

The Sun and the Pyramid: The only way to make the sun appear on the other side of the pyramid is to do this:

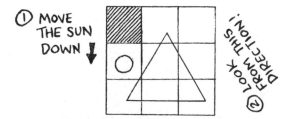

The Tongue Tank: The ladders are both 8 m long. We know the diameter of the tank is 10 so the radius is 5. If x is the length of the ladder you get a right-angled triangle like this:

Pythagoras tells you that $(\frac{x}{2})^2 + (x - 5)^2 = 5^2$. Multiply out the different bits and you get: $\frac{x^2}{4} + x^2 - 10x + 25 = 25$. Subtract 25 from each side and multiply the rest by 4: $x^2 + 4x^2 - 40x = 0$. You can divide everything in an equation by the same number providing it isn't zero. Obviously the ladders cannot be zero length, and therefore x cannot be zero. Therefore we can divide everything by x: to get $x + 4x - 40 = 0$. Move the bits round to get $5x = 40$; so $x = 8$.

Cockroach Café: The table numbered 17 in the very middle has 1 cockroach. As for the other tables, starting with the table numbered "2" and going round clockwise, they have 8, 2, 9, 11, 7, 4, 3, 12, 5, 10, 6 and 0.

The Secret Underground System: Pass these letters in order: DSTEFHWX.

Crocked Clocks: The time now is 5.30 which is shown on the Duchess's clock. The clocks were set at 8.00 (shown on Rodney's clock), 12.45 is Auntie Crystal's, 3.25 is the Colonel's, 10.30 is Binky's and 7.05 is Primrose's clock.

The Rat Race: Scabchops was last. The hint tells you that the moss eater won therefore the green rat came fourth. The bald rat isn't Gungie or Runt, and as it eats pizza boxes, it can't be Scratch. As Bubonic has no tail, Scabchops must be bald. Now see what the moss eater's feature is: the clues say it isn't bald, and they also tell us that the winner isn't one-eyed, spotty or green. Therefore the moss eater is the one with no tail which is Bubonic (who won). Now see what order the other features finished in. No-tail is first, the green rat is fourth, the clues say the one-eyed rat is third, and as the second rat eats slugs, it can't be the bald pizza-box eater: therefore, the second rat is spotty which leaves fifth place for the bald rat, which we've found out is Scabchops! Full results: **1** Bubonic – no tail – moss eater, **2** Runt – spotty – slug eater, **3** Scratch – one eyed – orange-peel eater, **4** Gungie – green – cheese-rind eater, **5** Scabchops – bald – pizza box eater.

97

The Devil's Dice

I know what your cheaty little brain is like – you won't have tried *any* of the puzzles properly. As soon as you got stuck you just looked the answer up and then said, "Oh, that was obvious." Well, you did, DIDN'T YOU? Yes you know you did, and the saddest thing is that now you've got to the end you actually believe you're rather clever, don't you?

Well, Smarty Bottom, allow me to introduce you to one final little brainbender...

Har har! It's not for nothing these are called the Devil's Dice! I know what you're thinking – which way up are the numbers supposed to be? Is it 18 or 81? Is it 89 or 68? Only I know that, and I also know that the two numbers on the bottom add up to 105.

Now let's see what happens when I pick them up and toss them again...

Oh dear! I'm not even sure which dice is which! Did I swap them over or didn't I? I don't know, but I will tell you this much: all twelve numbers on the dice are different. Oh, and this time the two numbers on the bottom add up to 149.

Just one more toss should do it…

There, you've seen enough. You can go away now. Go on, leave this book before your tears of frustration soak the pages and make them mouldy. There's no point in even attempting to answer my final challenge to you… What do the two numbers on the bottom of the dice now add up to?